CreateSpace Publishing: The Ultimate Easy & Fast

Step by Step Guide for Self Publishing!

By

Patrick Doucette

***

CreateSpace Publishing: The Ultimate Easy & Fast

Step by Step Guide for Self Publishing!

Table of Contents

Introduction

Congratulations on your decision to self-publish through Amazon! This book will guide you through the steps to get your written work onto the CreateSpace platform which in turn will allow your work to be made available as a real physical book! The default format will be as a 6" x 9" paperback but there are many other options for you as well, such as hardcover and as a digital Kindle edition.

The bonus section will cover more details on the Kindle publishing process as well strategies and methods to ensure that you get successful results for your writing efforts. So let's jump right in and get started!

Step 1

For this simple step by step plan, we are starting from the position that you already have your completed manuscript. Ideally this has been saved as a Microsoft Word document (.doc) on your desktop, notebook or portable device.

If you have not actually written your book yet, you will probably want to read the bonus section first for ideas about what to write about and how to choose a title, etc.

So first we go to the CreateSpace site at www.createspace.com

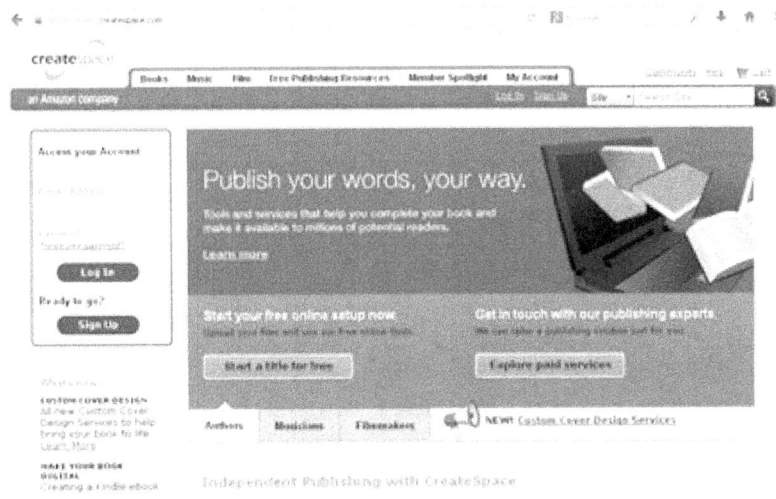

From the main screen, you simply sign up for a new account following the prompts. Once you have signed up, you log into your account which immediately takes you to your member dashboard. From your member dashboard, you click on the button that says "Add New Title" as in the image below:

That will take you to the next screen as in the image below:

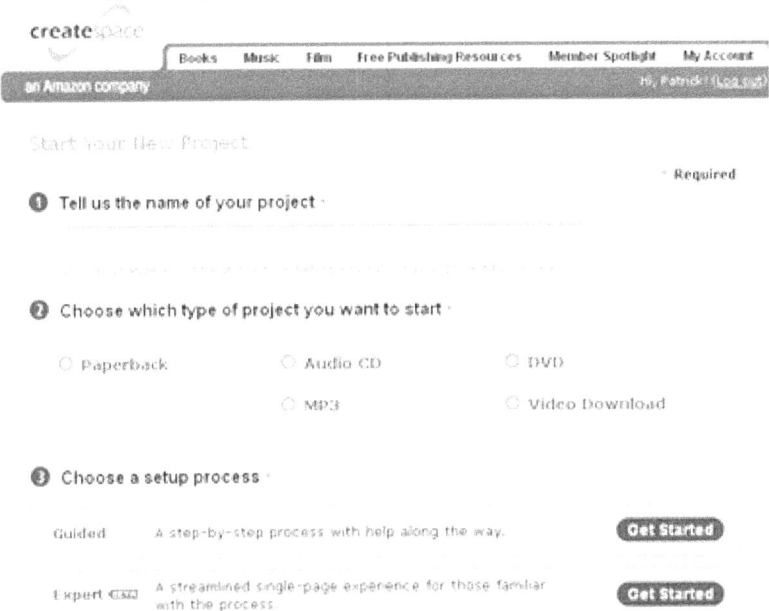

On this 'Title Information' screen, you simply fill in each section with the correct information. As indicated by the asterisks, the 'Title' and 'Primary Author' sections are mandatory and the rest are optional. Click on the Guided step-by-step 'Get Started' button at the bottom right corner of the screen to move to the next section.

Step 2

Now you will assign an ISBN number for your book. Click on the option 'Free CreateSpace-Assigned ISBN' as indicated by the arrow in the following image.

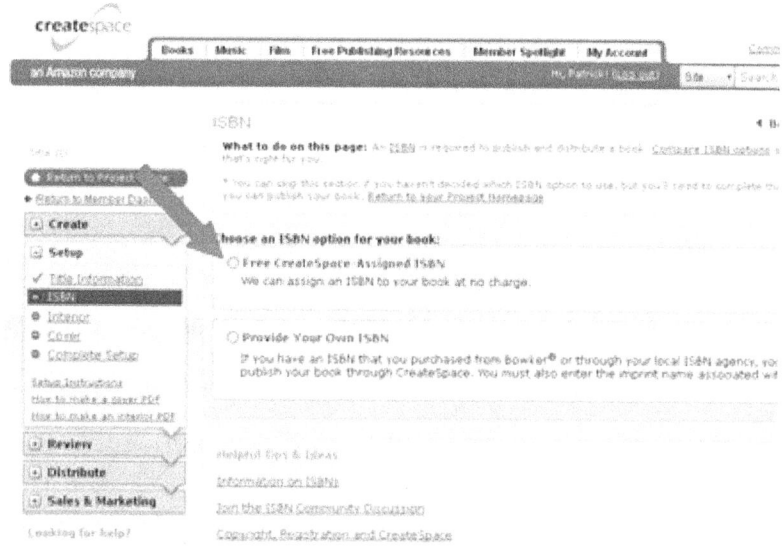

If you had an ISBN from elsewhere you would select the second option, 'Provide Your Own ISBN' but most likely you are starting fresh and will need to select the first option as indicated in the above image.

Scroll down and click on the 'Save & Continue' button; you will be taken to the following screen:

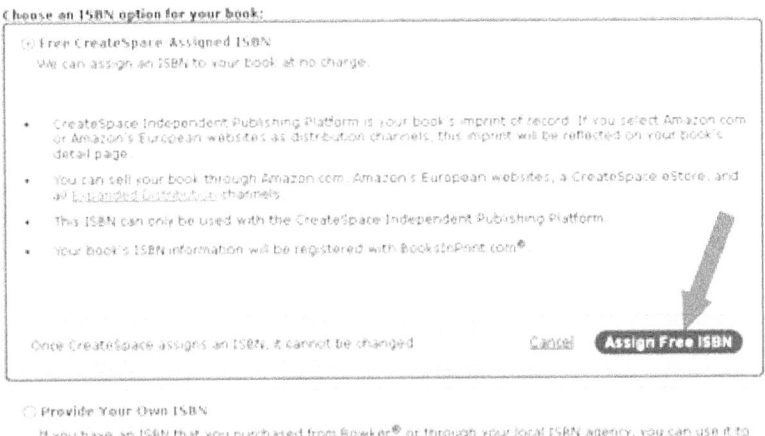

Click the button at the bottom right as indicated by the red arrow, 'Assign Free ISBN'. You will be taken to the next screen as in the image below:

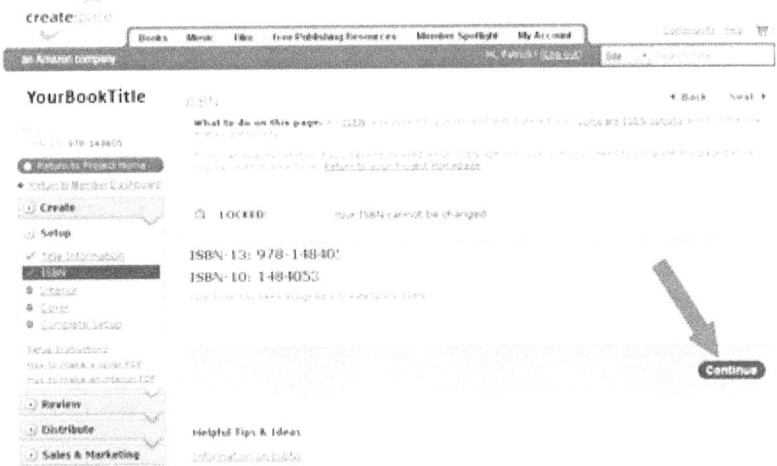

You will see the ISBN number(s) that have been generated for your book. You may want to write then down for reference. Now click the 'Continue' button as indicated by the red arrow in the previous image.

Step 3

You will now reach the section on creating the interior of your book as in the image below:

I would recommend staying with the default selections; that is, the black and white interior type and the 6" x 9" trim size. At this point you have the option to download a Word Template. They offer a blank template and a formatted template; you may want to download these for reference but they are not necessary if you follow the Word formatting guidelines that are detailed later.

Next click on the 'upload your book file' as in the image below and then click 'Save & Continue'.

Now you will reach a screen where you can actually upload your book manuscript:

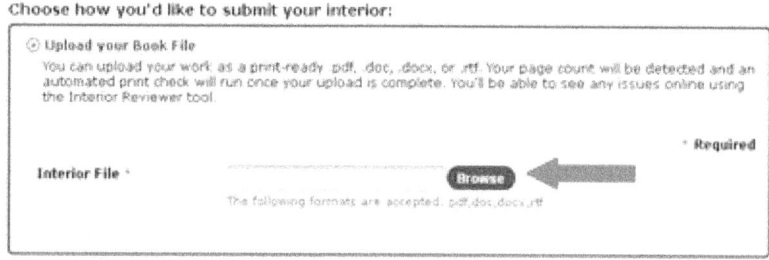

From this screen, you simply click 'Browse' and then locate the manuscript file on your computer. Once you locate the file, select it and click upload. As your manuscript file is uploading to CreatSpace, you will see a progress screen as in the image below:

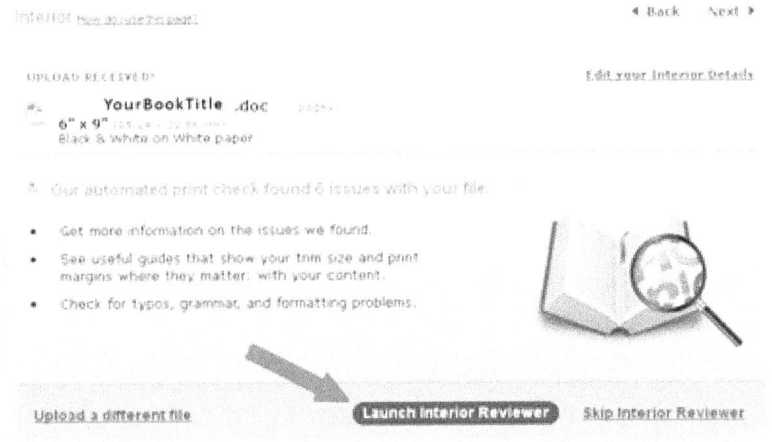

Choose how you'd like to submit your interior:

⦿ Upload your Book File
You can upload your work as a print-ready .pdf, .doc, .docx, or .rtf. Your page count will be detected and an automated print check will run once your upload is complete. You'll be able to see any issues online using the Interior Reviewer tool.

Required

Interior File

Browse
.pdf,.doc,.docx,.rtf

Uploading   93%

⦾ Talk with us about Professional Design Services
Starting at $249
Let us design and format your manuscript. Our experienced team can help with fonts, margins, chapter headings, and other eye-catching details to enhance the professional appearance of your book.

Save

Once your book has finished uploading, you be taken to the following screen:

Interior How do I use the tool?

◀ Back   Next ▶

UPLOAD RECEIVED!

Edit your Interior Details

YourBookTitle .doc
6" x 9"
Black & white on White paper

⚠ Our automated print check found 6 issues with your file.

• Get more information on the issues we found.
• See useful guides that show your trim size and print margins where they matter, with your content.
• Check for typos, grammar, and formatting problems.

Upload a different file

Launch Interior Reviewer

Skip Interior Reviewer

You will notice at the top it says, 'Upload Received!' At this point you will also notice that there is an alert message that indicates, "Our automated print check found issues with your file". Click on the "Launch Interior Reviewer" Button, where you will the following:

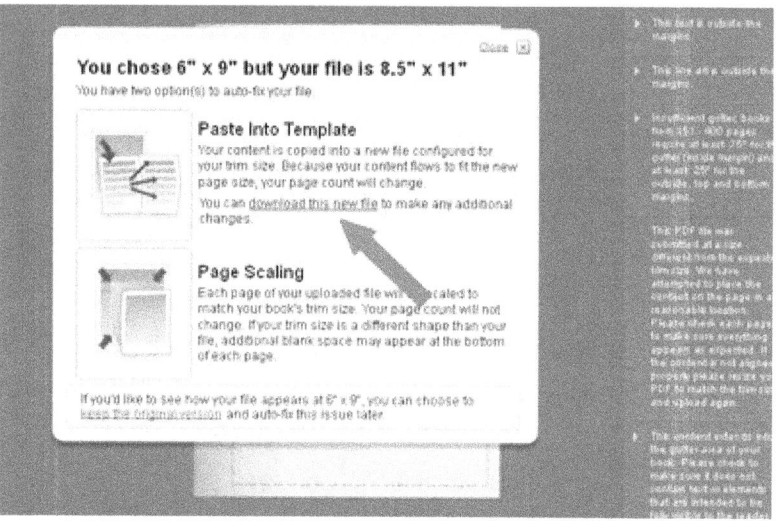

Now this step is very important: You will see the message that says, "You chose 6"x9" but your file is 8.5"x11" – your content is copied into a new file configured for your trim size – You can **download this new file** to make any additional changes. You must click this download option as indicated by the red arrow in the previous image.

Once you download this file, (corrected for 6"x9" format by Amazon for you) open it in Word and examine it for any formatting issues. If you are using the Word formatting guidelines included below, you should have no issues; you can go ahead and re-upload this newly formatted document.

Once you re-upload your document, you will see the following screen:

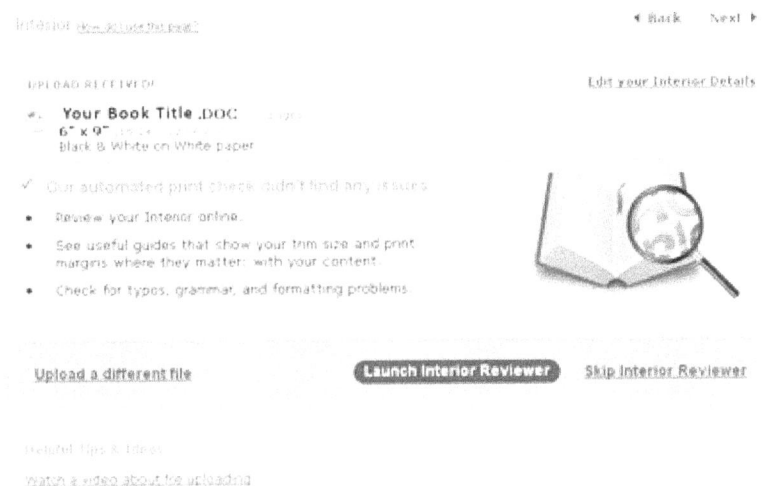

Now you should see the message: "Our automated print check didn't find any issues." If you still have some issues, you can launch the Interior Reviewer and correct any outstanding issues. The Interior Reviewer looks like the following:

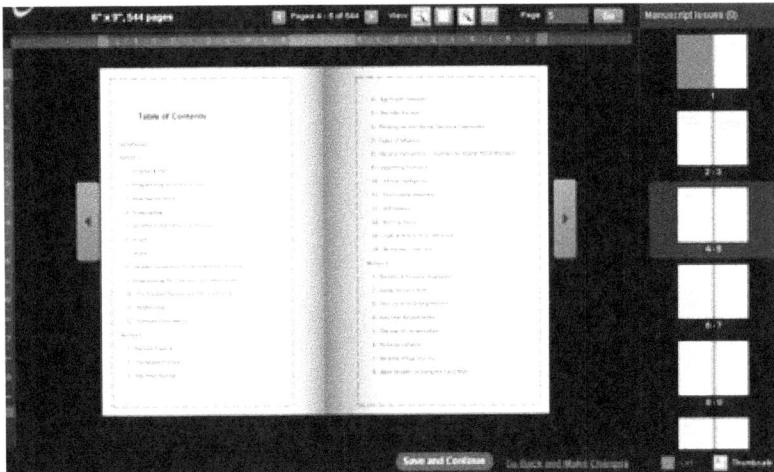

It allows you to flip through the pages of your book to make sure it looks correct. Images should be 400 pixels wide to avoid running off the edges of the pages. For any adjustments, you will need to re-upload your corrected file.

Step 4

Once you are satisfied with your manuscript upload, click save and continue to reach the next section; building your cover.

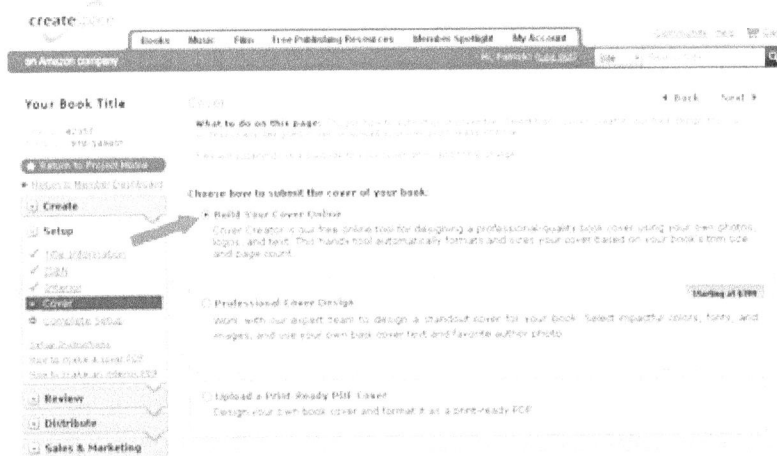

Click on the 'Build Your Cover Online' option as indicated in the above image. You can see that having a professional cover designed starts at $399. You also have the option to upload a print-ready PDF cover design if you already have one.

Once you choose the 'build your cover online' option , you will see the following screen:

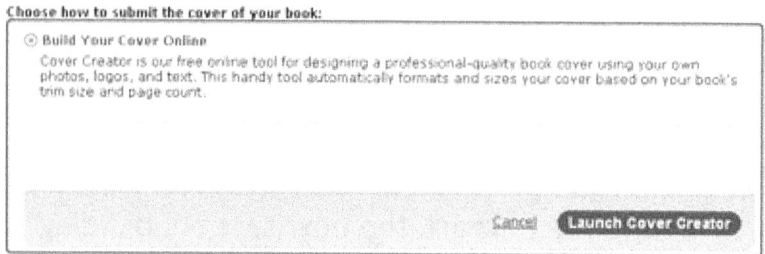

This is simply an additional prompt to start building your cover; click on the 'Launch Cover Creator' button at the bottom right.

Now you will a number of colorful cover templates for you to choose from.

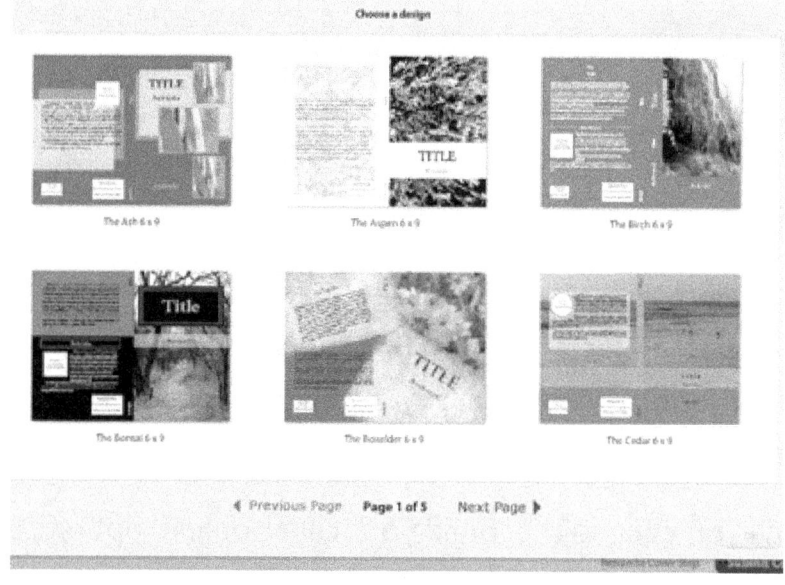

You can use these templates or you can add your cover images from your graphics program. I create covers using Photoshop so I will show you the steps I follow to upload my own cover images.

Within the Cover Creator section, click the next page prompt until you reach page 4 as in the image below:

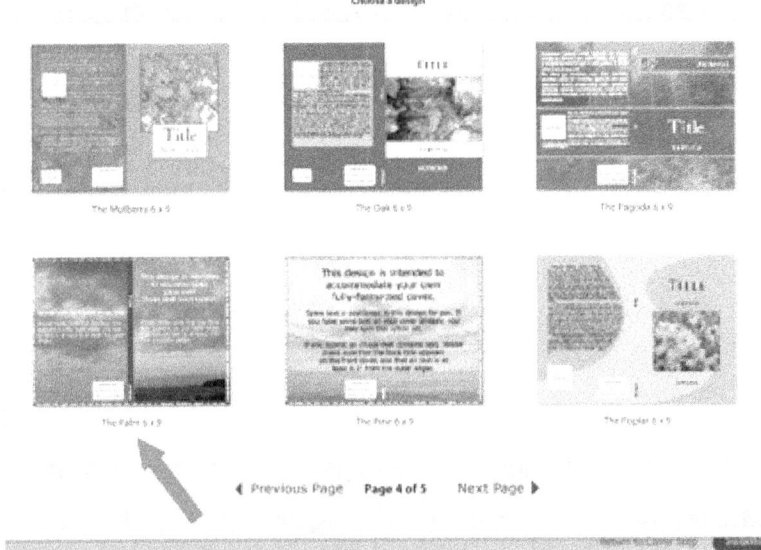

Now you will select the template called "The Palm 6 x 9" as indicated by the red arrow in the above image. This will take you to the template where you will be able to go through each section and add your graphics and text.

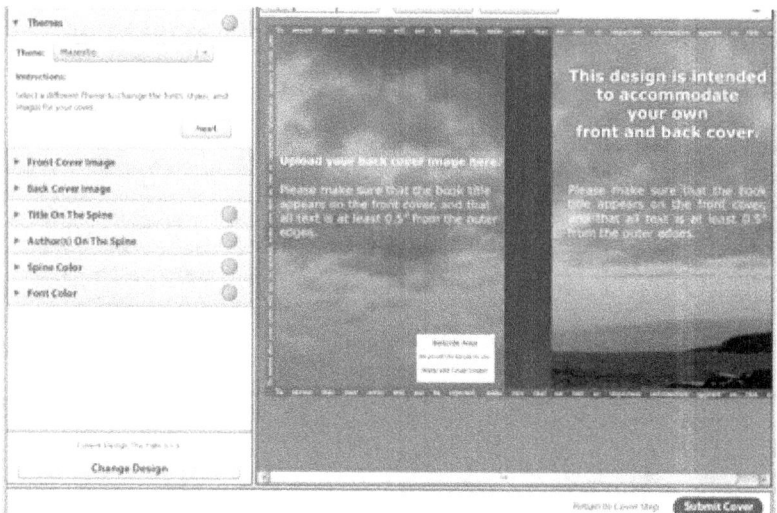

You simply follow each section on the left hand side to upload your front and back images, insert text for Title on the spine, insert text for Author on the spine, choose spine color and font color. When you are finished uploading your cover images and adding text, you hit the "submit cover" button in the bottom right hand corner. This will bring you to the following page:

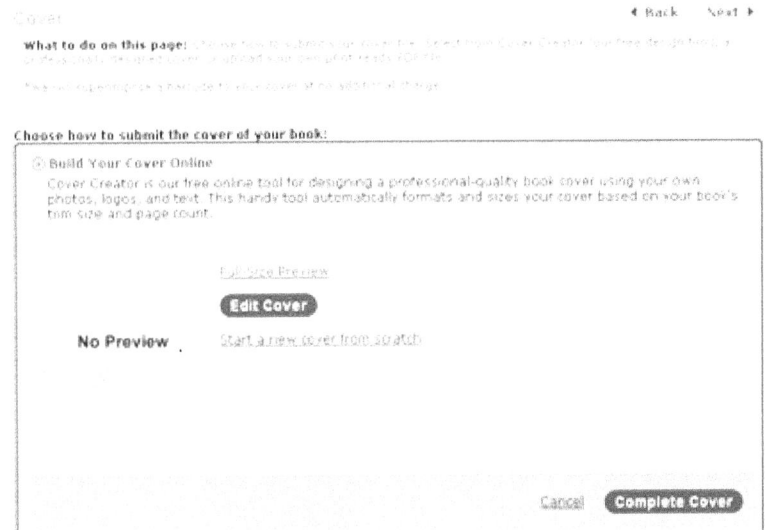

Sometimes the preview function will not work properly. You may need to go back and edit cover and then submit again or you can click on 'full-size preview' to get a preview of your cover. Once you are satisfied, click on the 'complete cover' button.

The next screen will allow you to confirm your cover upload. You can also open a full size preview from this screen.

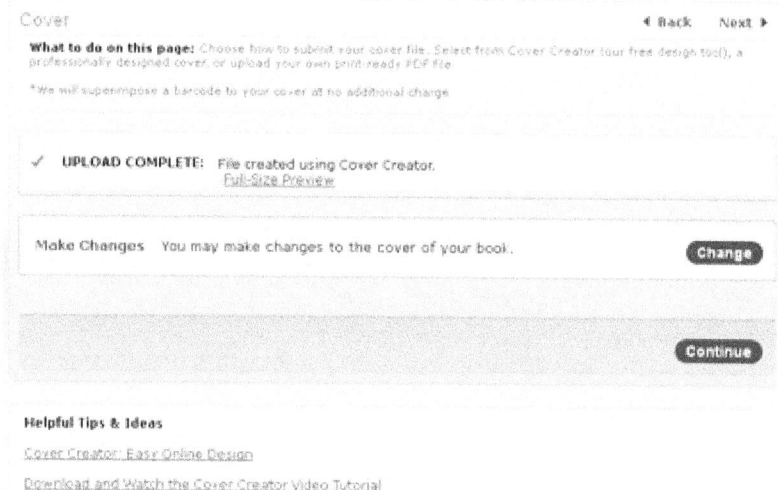

When satisfied with the cover, simply click on the 'continue' button in the bottom right corner.

Step 5

Now you reach a screen that will summarize your book files and tells you what happens when you submit them:

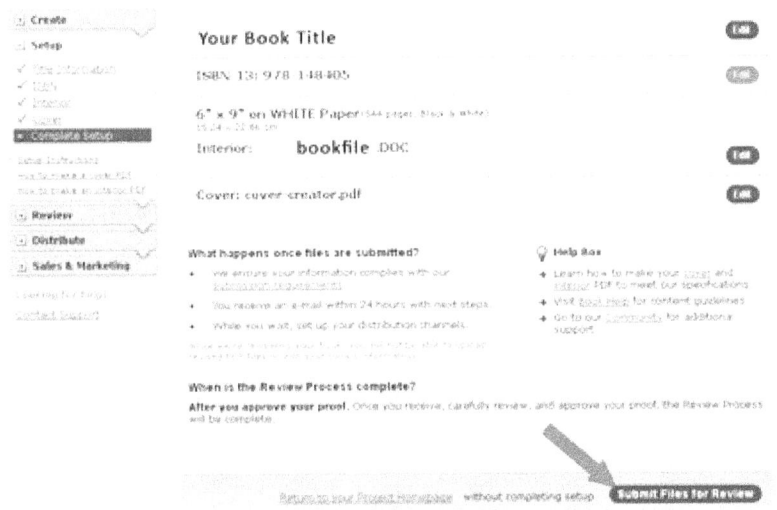

To complete the setup process, click on the 'submit files for review' button as indicated by the red arrow above.

Next you will be brought to a screen that shows the distribution channels:

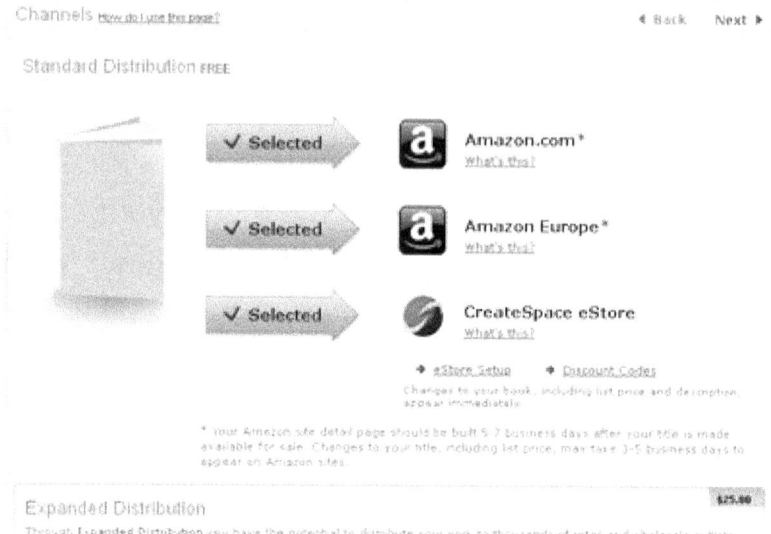

You also have the option to purchase expanded distribution for $25. I choose this option only if my books are selling more than $25 per month through the 3 free distribution channels.

Next you are brought to a screen that allows you to add your book description and category.

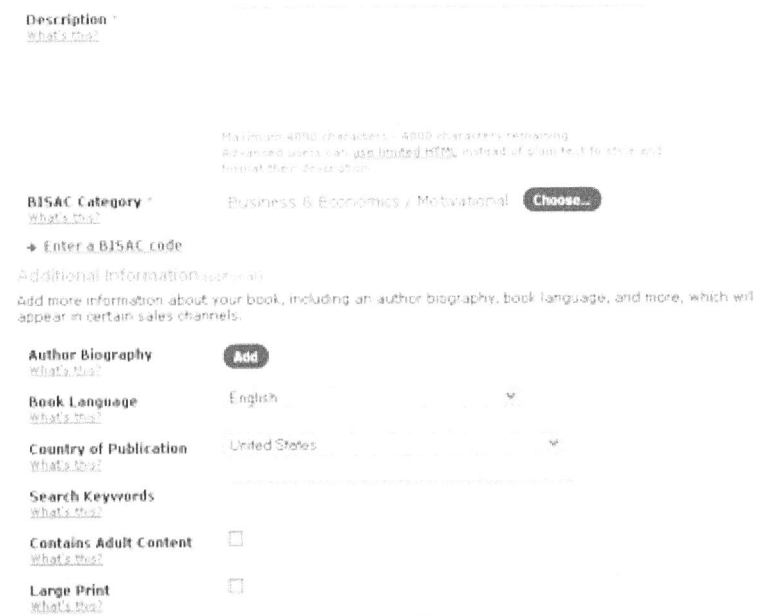

You book description should be compelling and effective in encouraging the reader to purchase your book. You should compare books that are similar to your own; and that are selling well; to get an idea of what constitutes a good description.

Once you are finished with your book submission to CreateSpace, you will have the option to also publish it to Kindle (KDP) from the CreateSpace platform.

Your book files are still being reviewed. A final print ready cover file is needed to continue to KDP. You will be e-mailed when the review is complete.

⟩ Take me to Kindle Direct Publishing now

How It Works

1 **We'll send your book to KDP.**
When you say the word, your book interior and cover files will be sent to KDP on your behalf and converted automatically for publication on Kindle.

2 **You'll sign in.**
We'll bring you to KDP where you will need to sign in with your Amazon account or create a new one

3 **You'll find your book.**
Your book will be waiting for you in your KDP Bookshelf. Check to make sure everything looks okay before

- Make your book available in more formats so your readers have more choices.
- Reach millions of readers on the Amazon Kindle Store.
- Participate in KDP's 70% royalty program.
- Publish your work to many countries around the world.

*Note: I would recommend to upload books to Kindle through the Kindle interface and NOT from the CreateSpace platform. I have found that when converting your CreateSpace files to KDP, things may get glitched up.

I always submit my files to CreateSpace and to KDP (Kindle) separately through their own platforms. Amazon automatically matches them to each other within about a week of them both being submitted.

That's it! You're done! At this point, you will have the option again to download your files for reference.

Want to download your book cover and interior files?
Here are the files we'll be sending to KDP - feel free to download them to your computer for safe-keeping

Kindle-Ready Book Cover

Your print cover is still being checked by our reviewers. You will be e-mailed when the review is complete.

Book Interior File

⬇ Download this file to my computer

Get Answers to Frequently Asked Questions about Publish on Kindle

How do I publish on KDP?

Why should I publish my book on KDP?

The next section will explain formatting in Microsoft Word and then you have the Bonus section talking about Selling on Kindle.

Formatting your manuscript in Microsoft Word

Authors sometimes have difficulty is getting their Word documents formatted properly so that they can upload to the Amazon Kindle platform. These pointers will make sure that your eBook will look good when customers read it using their Kindle devices.

*Remember when saving your Word document, you must save it as a (Word 97-2003) document. The file extension will then be .doc not .docx or any other format. This is the simplest format for uploading to either Kindle or CreateSpace. When Uploading this format in 8.5" x 11" size to CreateSpace, Amazon will automatically re-format it for you and provide a fresh file for you to re-upload.

If you are already familiar with uploading using html, pdf, docx or any other formats; that is fine; I am just telling you the simplest method that works fast.

1) Insert indents at the start point of each paragraph:

It is better not to use tabs and spaces to indent paragraphs. Set the "first line" indents (for paragraphs) in Word as follows:

Click on the "Page Layout" tab at the top of the screen in Word

In the bottom-right corner of the "Paragraph" section of this tab, click the button that resembles a downward pointing arrow

In the pop-up menu, find the "Indentation" section, and set "Special" to "First line" and "By" to your preferred indent (in the example below 0.5", which is the setting we recommend, if you want your first line to be indented).

2) Insert empty space between paragraphs:

If you insert a "return" (or carriage return) between two paragraphs you cannot be sure that the space between paragraphs will appear correctly on all Kindle platforms. Instead, set your paragraph spacing in Word as follows:

With your Word document open, click on the "Page Layout" tab at the top of the screen

In the "Paragraph" section of this tab, locate the section entitled "Indent"

Next to the word "After", you can enter a value for your preferred space after a paragraph (in the example below, Word will allow a 10 point space after a paragraph, before the next paragraph).

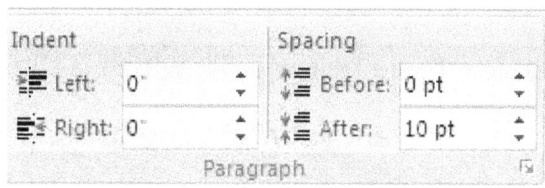

3) Insert page breaks between chapters:

Enter a page break at the end of every chapter to prevent the text from running together on Kindle. To insert a page break in Word:

Click "Insert" at the top of the screen in Word

Click "Page Break"

Images: Avoid pasting in images: Images should be inserted in JPEG (or .jpg) format with center alignment (don't copy and paste from another source).

Click "Insert" at the top of the screen in Word

Click "Picture", which brings up a dialogue screen to locate the picture that will be inserted in the document. Your pictures should be 400 pixels in width. Pictures that are 500 pixels in width will run off the page in the standard 6"x9" CreateSpace format.

In the dialogue screen, locate and select the file If your book has a lot of images, it can be viewed in color by readers using Kindle Fire or our free Kindle apps for PC, MAC, iPad, iPhone, and Android. Otherwise, remember that images on Kindle e-ink devices are displayed in 16 shades of gray.

Do not use headers and footers: Headers, such as title and chapter, and footers, such as page number, will not display on Kindle as intended; avoid using them.

Use Word's "Heading 1" formatting feature for chapters: Kindle will support easy navigation within your book for the reader if you highlight chapter titles (e.g., "Chapter 1") and set them to a "Heading" value as shown below.

In your manuscript, highlight the chapter title with your mouse

Click on the "Home" tab

Click on the "Heading 1" button as shown below

Your text will be formatted differently. You can change the formatting values for "Heading 1" to anything you wish by right-clicking on the same button and selecting "Modify". If you have already formatted your chapter headings the way you would like, you can highlight the heading, right-click on "Heading 1" and select "Update Heading 1 to Match Selection." After this, anything you set to Heading 1 will match the settings you selected.

Font size: Kindle readers can reconfigure the text size (i.e., font size) and margins while reading on Kindle. Because of this, you may wish to avoid utilizing font size to add emphasis.

Building the Front Matter of Your Book

The front matter is everything between your book's cover and first chapter. Front matter may include a title page, copyright page, dedication, preface or prologue. At minimum, your front matter should include a title page. Below are some tips to help make your front matter look stylish and professional.

Title page: The first page in your manuscript document should be your title page (you will upload your cover page, an image, separately when you publish your book). Your title page should be centered with the book title on top and the author name underneath. To center simply highlight text and click the center tab from the home screen.

Insert a page break after the title.

Click "Insert" at the top of the screen in Word   Click "Page Break"

Example:

The Book of Fun and Games By John Doe

- Insert Page Break Here –

Copyright

The copyright Page normally follows the title page. It should also be centered with a page break after it, as shown here.

Text copyright © 2012 John Doe All Rights Reserved

- Insert Page Break Here –

Dedication:

If your book has a customized Dedication, it should follow the Copyright Page. It should also be centered with a page break after it, as shown here:

To my wife and kids for their love and support

- Insert Page Break Here –

Preface:

If you have a Preface and/or Prologue, they should follow the Dedication. These can be formatted like any regular book chapter, and each of them should end with a page break. These should come after your table of contents, which is described in the next section. By inserting a page break after each of these front matter elements, you will be giving each of them, in order, their own starting page, resulting in a professionally sequenced opening portion for your book.

Building Your Table of Contents In a Kindle book, the Table of Contents allows readers to jump to pre-determined places in the book by simply clicking on links embedded in the text. As page numbers are not applicable in a Kindle book (page counts change with the text size a reader chooses), a functional Table of Contents is one of the features Kindle readers rely on and expect. Kindle will recognize a properly implemented Table of Contents in Microsoft Word. If your book is in Word, follow the steps below to ensure your table of contents works properly on Kindle.

1. Identify your chapter headings and set your heading style:
2. In your manuscript, highlight the first chapter title in your book with your mouse
3. Click on the "Home" tab
4. Click on the "Heading 1 Button as shown below

Your chapter title text will be formatted differently. You can change the formatting values for "Heading 1" to anything you wish by right-clicking on the same button and selecting "Modify"

If you have already formatted your chapter headings how you would like them to look, you can highlight the first one, right-click on "Heading 1" and select "Update Heading 1 to Match Selection."

Once you have set your chapter heading style, identify the rest of the chapter headings by repeating the first two steps above for each one.

Insert your table of contents near the beginning of the Word document o Left click once where you want your table of contents to appear. This should come just after your front matter (title page, dedication, etc.) Type "Table of Contents" and press Enter.

In Microsoft Word, locate the "References" tab at the top and find "Table of Contents"

Click "Table of Contents" and select "Insert Table of Contents..." from the drop down, which will cause a dialogue box to appear

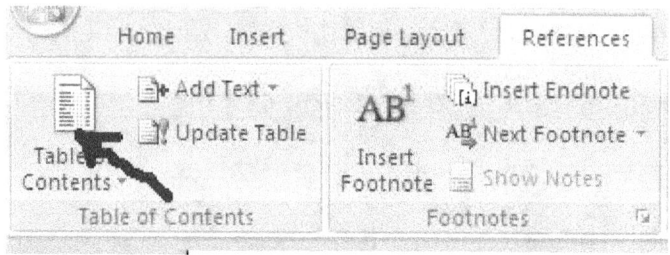

On the dialogue box, uncheck the box that says "Show Page Numbers" (since this is an e-book and page numbers will vary on the Kindle reader as the user changes font size) Set the "Show levels" box to 1

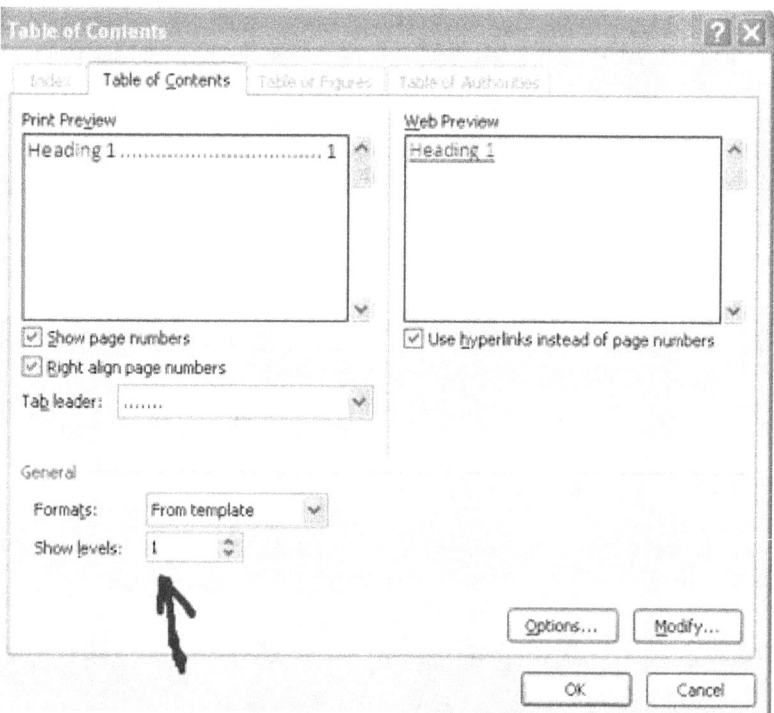

Click "OK". The table of contents should appear automatically. If you need sub-chapters in your table of contents you would need to select Show Levels: 2.

3. Set a bookmark so Kindle can find your Table of Contents Kindle offers readers the option to "Go To" certain places in a book such as the table of contents, cover, or the opening passage (such as chapter 1), from anywhere within the book. These places are known as "Guide Items." To identify your table of contents as a guide item, follow these steps: Highlight the words "Table of Contents" in your document , Click on the "Insert" tab and then Select "Bookmark".

4. Revisions: If you add more chapters (or chapter headings) to your book after completing instructions 1-3, make sure you identify them as "Heading 1" (as you did in step 1 above). To make sure your table of contents updates, click anywhere in your table of contents and hit the F9 key; this will add any new chapter headings and delete any removed ones. When you are done, you will have a professional quality table of contents that is properly created and situated within your document,

correctly identified and linked to your chapter headings, and available for users to "Go To" on demand.

BONUS SECTION:

Selling on Kindle: How to Boost Your Kindle Selling

With Proven Strategies that Work!

By

Patrick Doucette

Table of Contents:

Chapter 1 - A Brief Intro

Hi there and thank you for purchasing this eBook. I am going to provide you my simple and effective strategy for selling eBooks on Amazon Kindle as quickly as possible. You're going to get the straight goods that I am using today with no fluff and no filler! But before I start, I do think it would be helpful to tell you a bit about my own writing experience.

My first effort at writing was back in the year 2000. I had recently gone through a bitter break up with my ex and I thought writing would be a good form of therapy. I spent several months creating a 50,000 word book on personal investing. It had tons of valuable information with charts and diagrams galore. I felt I had created something of huge value that would appeal to a large target audience.

After a few rejections from business book publishers I decided to self-publish through a vanity publisher. At the time, that process was expensive and time consuming. Long story short, the book did not bring in the sales I had hoped. To be blunt, the sales sucked. Lesson learned, time to move on.

Fast forward to today and like you, I am hearing the 'buzz' about publishing to Kindle. Stories are starting to pop up about so and so and such and such making big sales here and there. So back I go; another book, another kick at the can and this time I get the same result; crickets chirping. This time however, I got my feedback a lot faster! Like almost instantly! So I simply asked myself, "Is there a way to discover what people are looking for and simply provide them some good quality eBooks on those topics?"

You see, a short while ago I had written a note to myself that reads: "The easiest way to fail is to try and provide what you think people want. The easiest way to succeed is to provide people what you know they want." That statement forced me to open my eyes to a simple method that allowed me to immediately start making consistent sales on Amazon that are continuing to improve every single day!

It took from hoping and wishing to actually doing. The beauty of Kindle is that you get almost instant feedback. If you are dreaming about being the next

Stephen King, you can waste a lot of time dreaming but if you want to put into action an iron-clad logic based system that gives people what they want; you've come to the right place.

My Super Simple Strategy WILL get you selling eBooks in record time. This is not theory; it is what I am actually implementing today, every day, and it is bringing me real significant sales. I am holding nothing back. I realize that the market is simply too massive to worry about anyone 'stealing' my methods. I want you to succeed! I know that if I give out, it comes back multiplied. You'll see in the video links that I explain everything in exact detail. All you have to do, is copy what I am doing and you can start making profits at your own pace. You may want to write one or two eBooks on your favorite topics. You may want to churn out a new eBook every month or more – you are only limited by your own goals and desires. This book will show exactly what I am doing and what I know works fast; so buckle up and hang on tight; the light is about to turn green……

Chapter 2 - My Super Simple Strategy That Works!

To sell eBooks effectively I started with the premise that the search function in Amazon works similar to the search function in Google. In other words I figure Google has already done all the work for me by finding out what people are looking for. This premise is likely not 100% correct but it's close enough to give me good results.

Step 1

The first thing I do is I use the Free Google Keyword tool available at:

https://adwords.google.com/o/KeywordTool

If you have an Adwords account with Google, you can simply sign in at the top right of the screen. If you don't have a Google account, it doesn't matter; you can still use it, but you simply have to enter the captcha request; whereas when you login, you can skip that step.

So here we are:

You simply type in the word or phrase that you want to write about or the word or phrase for which you already have an eBook manuscript.

If your word or phrase of interest returns a huge number of searches per month; you probably want to drill down into a more specific keyword. I like to target a keyword or phrase that has anywhere from a few thousand searches to 100,000 or even 200,000 searches per month but always less than 1 million. The reason this search number is so broad is because I want to compare number of searches to the number of current listing already available under that search phrase.

For example if the number of searches is 50,000 per month and there are only 100 titles available when I type in that search phrase on Amazon, that would definitely indicate good potential. If there are 100,000 searches per month but there are already over 1000 titles that come up on Amazon under that search term, I would likely shy away from trying to compete on that search term title.

For example if I type in the word 'Kindle' on the Adwords free keyword tool, it returns over 16 million searches per month. It would be next to impossible to achieve any kind of ranking on Amazon for that term.

However if I type in the word 'Kindle Template', it returns only 3600 searches per month and identifies it as a low competition keyword. This would be relatively easy to get ranked on the first page of search results. When I type in the phrase 'kindle template' on Amazon I get less than 500 search results so I figure I can target this keyword phrase for a title.

Let's look at another example. If I type in the phrase make money; it shows there are about 5 million searches per month. Too high. If I type in the phrase, 'make money online fast', it only has about 33,000 searches per month and even though it is a high competition keyword, I could probably still be able to rank on the first page of search results for that term. Are you starting to get the idea? Very basic right? Find what people are looking for is step one. <u>Start to think of using keyword phrases for your titles.</u>

Step 2

Next I head over to the Amazon Bestseller list page here:

http://www.amazon.com/gp/bestsellers/digital-text/154606011

Here we are:

Then I start typing in my search term from step one in the search box as in the above diagram.

You can see that as you type, Amazon lists suggested search terms based on what it knows customers have searched for in the past. If I start typing in K-I-N-D-L-E T-E-M-P...once I reached this point I can see that Kindle Template is selectable from the drop down list of selectable search terms. I select that term and hit 'Go'. It returns 438 results; a very reasonable number to compete against.

I can compete reasonably well against any term that has less than 1000 books for that particular search term. Even the term 'Make Money Online' is extremely competitive, I was able to rank in the top 15 search results right away with no sales and no reviews. It immediately got a few sales so I expect it will slowly move up in the ranking over time.

Step 3

From the returned search results from step 2 above, I check and see if the exact search term is contained in the title of any of the listed eBooks available. If it isn't, I know I have a winner. I now know that if I want to, I can create an eBook and **by using that search term in**

the title, I can be confident that my eBook will appear on the first page of search results with little or no promotion, no reviews and even prior to making any sales! How is that possible? Simple, think about it, Amazon wants to give customers what they want. If customers are searching for a Kindle Template and there are a number of book available like the following:

1 -Super Simple Solution to Format eBooks

2 -Kindle Template

3 -How to Prepare Your eBook for Kindle in 5 Easy Steps

The second book is the one with the 'worst' title but guess what? That's what the customer wants! And that is exactly why the second book will easily get ranked for that search term and the others will be buried who knows where. Makes sense right? You may have the better book but until you get tons of sales and reviews Amazon doesn't know that yet. If you want to get ranked fast you need to use the above short-cut to immediately get in front of what customers are searching for.

By the way, I notice that my book entitled 'Kindle Template' is now the #1 Book that comes up under the search term 'Kindle Template.' (it is under my name Patrick Doucette)

The temptation would be to name your ebook something snazzy like. "How to easily format your eBooks for Kindle" or "A Simple Kindle Template Solution." But that is not the best method for quick and direct results. I named the book 'Kindle Template' not because it is a nice sounding title but because that is what people want and are looking for.

I told you my strategy was super simple and I wasn't kidding! You can see how I put this to use in the videos in Chapter 4. Very easy to follow. You can use this strategy to complement whatever else you may be doing. This strategy is getting me good sales **before** I am using any other marketing methods. I have had very few if any reviews posted for my eBooks as of yet. I have not been blogging about my eBooks. I have not used any Tweets nor any paid or free advertising. I have simply been creating the content and then following the above simple steps.

If I would include a Step 4 it would be to include a simple bold cover design. I bought a collection of cover templates from fiverr.com for $5. You may want something more professional but wherever you get your covers, I recommend getting the PSD files so that you can easily and quickly modify them yourself using Photoshop.

Again, I recommend watching the videos so that you can clearly see how I am putting these steps into practice.

Chapter 3 - How to Format Your Description Page for Maximum Impact

To improve the look of your book description on Amazon, it's nice to be able to modify the font a bit so your description stands out.

If you try and type in regular HTML into the description area when you are uploading your work to Kindle, it will not appear correctly. Here is how to type in your description properly so that it will look right on Amazon's website:

To write your text in bold:

<b> Your Title </b>

You can see it looks very strange compared to regular HTML which would be written as:

<b> Your Title </b>

Amazon recognizes < as the left bracket and > as the right bracket so you can see it easy to make a mistake when trying to type these into the description. The best is just to cut and paste from this page and then change Your Title to whatever text you want to appear. Be careful since if you make a mistake, you will have to re-submit your description to your Bookshelf and then wait 12 to 24 for Amazon to update your corrections.

So here are a list of formatting styles you can use:

BOLD

<b> Your Title </b>

ITALICS

<i> Your Title </i>

Centered

<center> Your Title </center>

Amazon Orange Heading

<h2> Your Title </h2>

Large Heading

<h1> Your Title </h1>

You can play around with other formatting but best is to keep it simple to avoid errors. If you make a mistake, the result will be an embarrassing mess that will take you about a day to fix. If you are familiar with html then you can combine formatting as long as you are careful. For example you could make an Amazon Orange Heading that is also centered by using the following format:

<center><h2>Your Title </h2> </center>

You get the idea. You can also practice by formatting different sections of your description different and then watching how it turns out on the Amazon live website

To add an image into your description, you simply need the url of where the image is located. Best is to upload any desired image to your own webhost so you know it won't get deleted. Then add the following to your description where you want the image to appear.

<img src="http://www.yourdomain/images/yourpicture.jpg" />

If you want the image to be on the left with text wrap, use the following:

<img src="http://www.yourdomain/images/yourpicture.jpg" align="left" />

Of course you simply replace the http location in the above example with the location of your image.

Something that I include in my book description that I believe is very important.

Did you know that the vast majority of people searching Amazon books do not have a Kindle? And yet these same buyers can purchase your eBook and read it on their Desktop PC.

Include a line in your description explaining this to your customer. It can only increase your sales. This is also explained in more detail in video number 4 below.

Chapter 4 - A Video is Worth a Thousand Words!

As always you need to take action if you want to get sales on Kindle. I have always found video training to be extremely helpful in getting me motivated and allowing me to understand what's going on. Here are some excellent videos that show me putting these strategies to work.

*NOTE: If you are reading this in paperback and cannot click the links, you can visit YouTube and search for mrbehappy777, this will pull up the list of videos for you without having to type in the individual links.

Video #1

http://www.youtube.com/watch?v=trNVKrU11AE

Video #2

http://www.youtube.com/watch?v=FbnQ3xjoh-Y

Video #3

http://www.youtube.com/watch?v=nsbNJJFgwGk

Video # 4 http://youtu.be/YXovqflut-A

Video #5

http://www.youtube.com/watch?v=pDw0wSXVqHw

Video # 6

http://www.youtube.com/watch?v=Qf9vJp9fdDA

Grab a coffee, relax and follow along the above videos so you can replicate my strategy to your benefit!

Chapter 5 – A Word about Cookbooks

Most training and advice about selling on Kindle will tell you NOT to publish cookbooks or recipe books. There is a good reason for this. Most recipes are freely available already on the web and so it stands to reason that Amazon does not want you to simply copy and paste what is already available for free.

That being said, there is a very simply strategy that I have used and I would recommend for you so that you can produce high quality, 100% original content.

Most people know somebody that is a good cook and or somebody that is proud of their own unique cooking abilities. If you know somebody like that, simply ask them if you can partner up for a day or two to create a cookbook! If they are a close friend or a relative, they will likely be open to the idea; it is a fun and exciting way to spend a day!

I have a dear friend who is a great cook. I asked her if I could visit to document a few of her recipes. I told her I wanted to make a cookbook and would gladly share any proceeds with her. I brought a notebook and my very basic digital camera. All I had to do was follow her around, take lots of notes and snap lots of photos.

You see most cookbooks out there, you know the coffee table type; are filled with photos but often they do not follow a thorough step by step photo documentary style. They often have maybe one or two photos of ingredients and then a beautifully staged photo of the finished dish. That's great, but why not make a book that has twenty step by step photos for a cooking klutz like me!

By taking lots of pictures, you can create a more valuable cookbook that readers will enjoy and that they will be able to follow. You will also be providing totally unique and original contents. Your detailed notes can be transcribed in a style that is naturally descriptive and helpful.

By following this method, I was amazed at how fast the content piled up. In fact if you follow this method, you will want to make sure that you transcribe your notes quickly or you may easily forget the process due to a large volume of details.

I've created a video that describes this process for you here:

Video # 7 http://youtu.be/6OLLC0rH7gl

Chapter 6 - My Secret Source of Thousands of eBooks!

So what if you want to sell on Kindle but just totally suck as a writer? You start a topic and get distracted or procrastinate over and over again until you are ready to quit the whole idea altogether. Don't despair! There is still hope for you yet!

What if you had a source of thousands of eBooks that are in the public domain and that are free to download? Not only that, but what if you could download in different formats and they were all arranged for you by category and genre? How sweet would that be? Well now you have it:

http://www.manybooks.net

This little know site is chock full of Books that you can download and re-sell. Of course most will already be available on Amazon, in fact a lot of them will be available as free downloads so it would be pointless to try and re-submit them to Kindle. However there are still lots of gems in there that you can download for quotes, reference or simply to get your own creative juices flowing.

You can add your own introduction or make 'workbook versions' for any of these titles.

Go nuts! Use the advanced search feature and find the titles that interest you. Important point to remember: Let's say you find a free download of a book that is in the public domain and you want to upload it to Kindle. First check if the book is already offered for free. (It is just silly to try and sell books that are already free!) Second realize that you must add your own unique contribution to the work to differentiate it; that is, you must annotate it, illustrate it or otherwise contribute to the work so that Kindle will accept it. Personally I much prefer original content but I also have some public domains works that I have published to Kindle that are selling nicely so I would not discourage you if really want to sell a title that you like. Simply make sure to follow the guidelines detailed by Kindle exactly and you will have no problems.

Also make sure you follow the previously mentioned keyword tool research exercise above. That is, plug the title of your public domain work into the free keyword and find out how many people are searching for that title per month. If it is so obscure that very few people are searching for that title, don't waste your time going to the trouble of formatting it, annotating it, creating a cover and uploading it. It will simply not pay off.

A brief word about PLR. If you have been thinking of using PLR content (that is Private Label Rights) for your eBook content don't do it! Amazon does not allow you to upload books that are PLR or duplicate content of what is already available for free on the web. They do this to prevent a bad experience for the purchaser. If you do have content that you nor sure about make sure that you:

1) Completely new and unique title.

2) All new chapter titles.

3) Totally re-arranged content.

4) Completely re-written content into your own words.

5) Additional unique content added.

That number 4 is the big one. Make sure that the content
is unique!

You can use good quality PLR only for your
framework. The point is, don't deceive yourself. If you
think you can slap together a PLR book in a few hours
from crap source material, you are just kidding yourself.
Your Kindle customers will demand good quality, Kindle
corporate will demand it and if you're anything like me
you will likely demand it from yourself.

Nobody wants to buy a book that is shoddy and
besides you really cannot fake unique material. By going
the extra mile and providing a book of value, you can have
something you will be proud of that will provide long term

residual income. Change the phrase, "work once, get paid forever" to "Work Hard once, get paid forever!"

Put in the effort and you will reap the reward. Anyone reading this eBook for example will immediately know that it is genuine! They can watch the videos and see me actually explaining what I am doing.

If I tried to provide a PLR book about selling on Kindle without unique content, I would simply just fall flat on my face.

I hope that makes sense for anyone that may be thinking about PLR content.

Chapter 7 - The Top 100 eBook Topic Target List

Please note, these are my personal collection that I am providing to help spur your mind to new ideas. I make no claim as to whether they are in proper order according to actual popularity or demand! Except of course the first topic which has been a top seller for who knows how long!

MY TOP 100 NICHES IDEAS FOR TARGETING eBOOKS

1.) Sex (Shades of Grey type stuff)

2.) Fantasy (Harry Potter type stuff)

3.) Romance (soft stuff)

4.) Science Fiction

5.) Horror & Vampire stuff

(The above 5 categories I do not deal with at all but there are still tons of areas on non-fiction, see below- that you may enjoy writing about!)

6.) General Health & Fitness

7.) Drama

8.) Weight Loss

9.) Classic Books

10.) Children's Books

11.) Specific Health Cures (diabetes, cancer, etcetera)

12.) Biographies

13.) Make Money Online

14.) Cooking books

15.) Beauty

16.) Humor

17.) Relationships

18.) Espionage/Spy Novels

19.) Religious Books

20.) Mystery –Detective Stories

21.) Pets

22.) Sports

23.) Historical books

24.) Personal Finance

25.) Language Guides

26.) Gambling

27.) Personal Development

28.) Real Estate

29.) Travel & Leisure

30.) Anti Aging Ideas

31.) Copywriting

32.) Gay/Lesbian Issues

33.) Education

34.) Mobile Marketing

35.) Video Game stuff

36.) Politics

37.) Scientific Discovery

38.) Mortgage stuff

39.) Art Books

40.) Specific Dating Tips

41.) Loans/Debt Relief

42.) Forex

43.) Westerns

44.) Nature Books

45.) Government

46.) Economics

47.) Conspiracy Theories

48.) Internet Marketing

49.) Short-Story Collections

50.) SEO Tactics

51.) Poems

52.) Music

53.) Jogging

54.) Consulting

55.) Computer topics

56.) Software guides

57.) Pirate Stories

58.) Bodybuilding

59.) War Stories

60.) Anti-Virus Repair

61.) Web-Hosting

62.) Celebrities

63.) Hair Growth

64.) Hair Removal

65.) Automotive

66.) Surveys

67.) Occult

68.) Coupon Clipping

69.) Scrapbooking

70.) Affiliate Marketing

71.) Email Marketing

72.) Social Media Topics

73.) Meditation

74.) Philosophy

75.) Yoga

76.) Etiquette

77.) The Stock Market

78.) Mind Power

79.) Satire

80.) Satellite TV

81.) Organic Farming

82.) Martial Arts

83.) Hypnosis

84.) Tattoo Life

85.) Gothic Genre

86.) Freelancing

87.) Outsourcing

88.) Pay Per Click

89.) MLM

90.) Movies

91.) Networking

92.) Alcoholism

93.) Motorcycles

94.) Boating

95.) Photography

96.) Advertising

97.)   Web Design

98.)   Fashion

99.)   Lottery

100.) Astronomy/Space

Use the above categories to get your mind moving; what do I know a lot about? What can I easily write about? How can I help someone in one of the above categories? What topic is huge but is not even on the list above? The sky's the limit when it comes to topics that you can write about and quickly get good exposure.

Chapter 8 - Bonus Graphics for Your eBook Cover

Here is a download link to a free banner graphic that you can use to spice up your eBook covers. It includes the PSD file so if you have Photoshop, you can easily modify it to suit your needs.

http://www.patrickdoucette.com/images/banners.zip

If you have any problem accessing the links feel free to send me an email at:

contact@patrickdoucette.com

That winds up this eBook; short sweet and to the point! You can see that I have held nothing back, you now have the potential to easily surpass my efforts. All it takes is action on your part. Kindle publishing is currently a golden opportunity and I am guessing it will continue to be a great opportunity for anybody that is committed to providing value and is willing to put in the effort to succeed. You can do it! Don't give up!

Thank you again for purchasing this eBook, I hope you have great success selling on both Kindle and CreateSpace!

www.ingramcontent.com/pod-product-compliance
Lightning Source LLC
Chambersburg PA
CBHW070556290526
45790CB00002B/714